Magic Carpet for Viola

Concert Pieces for the Youngest Beginner

by Joanne Martin

ISBN 0-7390-4624-1

INTRODUCTION

Magic Carpet is a collection of audience-pleasing concert pieces for the youngest beginners. These pieces can be used in either a reading-based or a Suzuki teaching environment, and teachers can choose whether the children learn them by reading or by ear. *Magic Carpet* is available for violin, viola, and cello students, with a separate book, piano accompaniment, and CD for each instrument.

Young children often take many months to learn the skills necessary to play their first pieces. *Magic Carpet* provides an opportunity to work on basic technical skills in an enjoyable musical context, skills such as tone production, rhythm, ensemble playing, string crossings and finger placement. As children refine these skills their confidence and musicality grows, and they build a strong foundation for future musical development.

The pieces in *Magic Carpet* use the same rhythms as the Twinkle Variations in the *Suzuki Viola School Volume 1*. The first eight pieces in the book are played on open A, and have an optional melody part, which may be played by teachers or more advanced students. This melody part is transcribed for violin and cello, to facilitate mixed-instrument ensembles. These transcriptions can be found on pages 14-29 of the viola book. *Magic Carpet* also includes five pieces which are designed to develop string crossings and finger placement.

The viola and cello versions of *Magic Carpet* are a fifth lower than the violin version. In mixed teaching situations where there are beginners on violin in addition to viola or cello, it is best to use the piano accompaniment and CD for the viola or cello version, and to have the young violinists play on open A instead of open E.

The titles of the pieces suggest the rhythms to be played, and each title contains a place name. Some information on each place is included in the Teachers' Notes, and children may enjoy looking up more information with their parents or teachers.

On the CD each piece is recorded at two speeds, with all the pieces played at the faster tempo first. Then all pieces are played at a slower tempo, for beginners who want to play along with the CD.

During the development of *Magic Carpet*, numerous friends, colleagues, and students have provided a wealth of helpful feedback. Particular thanks go to Carey Cheney, Dorothy Conoghan, David Dunford, Christie Felsing, Chantal Latil, Carolyn McCall and Patricia Shand for all the time and thought they put into their comments and suggestions.

I owe a huge debt of gratitude to cellist Karin Erhardt and pianist Carole Pollard, who recorded the CD's with me. Their invaluable ideas helped make the piano and cello parts more user-friendly, and the entire project was greatly enriched by their musicality, friendship and sense of humour. Many thanks also go to recording engineer Bryan Harder for his patience, perfectionism and technical wizardry.

As with all my projects, I am extremely grateful to my husband Peter and my daughter Shauna for their cheerful encouragement, creative ideas, patience, and unquestioning support.

Magic Carpet is dedicated to Edmund Sprunger, whose idea it was to write a series of pieces for beginners, and who has been so generous with his wisdom from start to finish of the project.

I hope that many children will enjoy flying on this Magic Carpet to their chosen musical destinations.

Joanne Martin

Contents

Wintertime in Russia

Joanne Martin

Carnival in Rio

Joanne Martin

Santiago Sunshine

Joanne Martin

Tango to Trinidad

Joanne Martin

Dancing in Avignon

Joanne Martin

Bow River Fiddling

Joanne Martin

Honolulu Hula-Dancer

Joanne Martin

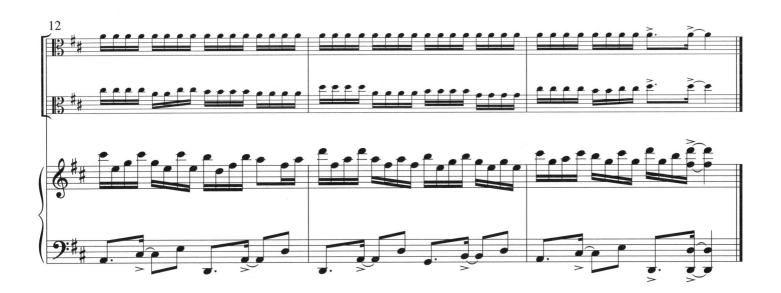

Chopsticks in Chinatown

Euphemia Allen
Arranged by Joanne Martin

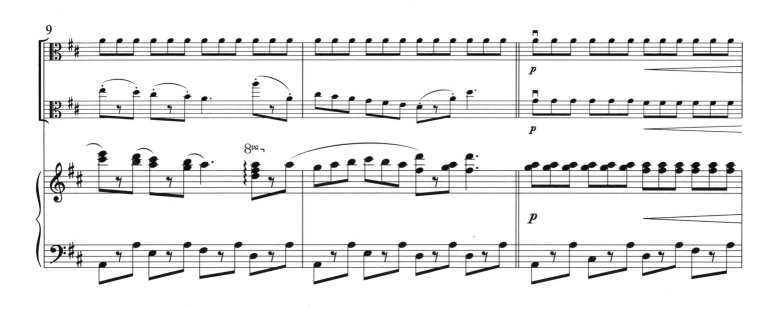

Atacama Crossing

Joanne Martin

Cross Lake Blues

Joanne Martin

Darling River Monkey

Joanne Martin

Athabasca Monkey

Joanne Martin

Machu Picchu Mountain

Joanne Martin

TEACHERS' NOTES

The first eight pieces in *Magic Carpet* can be played as solos or duets. Each of these pieces has a part played on open A, an optional melody part for more advanced players, and a piano accompaniment. Many teachers will have their students learn the open A part by ear, in which case the children will need to pay attention at the end of each piece, since frequently the rhythm changes for the last measure. These eight open string pieces use the rhythms from the Twinkle Variations in the *Suzuki Viola School*, and should be played with short bow strokes, stopping the bow after each eighth note. The melody (viola 2) parts have been transcribed for violin and cello, to make it possible to have an ensemble of any combination of instruments. The violin and cello parts can be found on pages 14-29 of the viola book.

The last five pieces in *Magic Carpet* have one viola part, and these pieces develop the skills of string crossings and finger placement. Many teachers will also have their students learn these pieces by ear.

Wintertime in Russia
Russia is the largest country in the world, stretching from eastern Europe to Asia. It is also the coldest country in the world, with approximately one half of its area covered in permafrost. Although the most commonly spoken language is Russian, over one hundred other languages are spoken. "Wintertime in Russia" should evoke images of dancers in colorful costumes, twirling and kicking their legs high to energetic music. "Wintertime in Russia" should be played near the middle of the bow, using very small bow strokes, with a clean resonant stop after each eighth note.

Carnival in Rio
Rio de Janeiro is Brazil's second largest city after São Paulo, and is famous for its beautiful location on the waterfront, for its beaches, for the giant statue of *Cristo Redentor* (Christ the Redeemer) overlooking the city, and for its Carnival celebrations. Rio de Janeiro in the local Portuguese language means "river of January". Carnival is a public street party and celebration, which takes place in many parts of the world immediately before the Christian season of Lent. In Rio de Janeiro, Carnival is famous for its samba dancing. "Carnival in Rio" should be played with very little bow, with clean stops after each eighth note.

Santiago Sunshine
Santiago, the largest city in Chile, is located on a plateau near the Andes mountains, and has a Mediterranean climate with hot sunny summers. There are cities called Santiago in other countries as well, including Panama, Cuba, and the Dominican Republic, plus Santiago de Compostela in north-western Spain. "Santiago Sunshine" should be played with very small strokes in the middle of the bow, stopping the bow after each eighth note. Players need to watch the leader for the "cha-cha-cha" at the end.

Tango to Trinidad
Trinidad is an island in the southern Caribbean sea, part of the republic of Trinidad and Tobago. The tango is a dance which originated in Buenos Aires, Argentina, and became popular internationally in the early twentieth century. It is known for its characteristic rhythms and dramatic dance moves. All eighth notes in the viola parts should be played with a ringing staccato, with the bow stopping cleanly after each note.

Dancing in Avignon
Avignon is a city in the south of France. Children around the world sing *"Sur le pont d'Avignon, on y danse, on y danse"* ("on the bridge of Avignon people dance, people dance"). The bridge in the song is the Pont Saint Bénezet, which was partly destroyed in a flood in the year 1660. It was never rebuilt, and now spans only half of the Rhone river. All eighth notes should be played with a short bow stroke, stopping the bow so that the sound rings after each note.

Bow River Fiddling
The Bow River (pronounced like the bow we use to play viola) flows from the Rocky Mountains of Alberta, Canada, through Banff National Park and Calgary. There is a strong tradition of fiddling in Alberta. "Bow River Fiddling" should be played with a small amount of bow and with all eighth notes staccato. In the melody (viola 2) part, be careful to move the first finger backwards for the B flat in the "shave and a haircut" ending.

Honolulu Hula-Dancer

Honolulu is the capital city of Hawaii, in the south Pacific. The Hula is a traditional Hawaiian dance which was originally religious in origin, and which through the years has evolved into a popular symbol of Hawaii. Dancers typically wear grass skirts and leis (chains of flowers) around their necks, ankles, and wrists. Frequently the hula is accompanied by ukulele, steel guitar, and bass. In "Honolulu Hula-Dancer," players should use a small amount of bow throughout. Listening to the piano part will help the ensemble stay together.

Chopsticks in Chinatown

The well-known piano piece called "Chopsticks" has nothing to do with the Chinese eating utensil. The piece was written by a 16-year old British schoolgirl named Euphemia Allen and published in 1877 under the pseudonym of Arthur de Lulli. Its original title was "The Celebrated Chop Waltz," probably because the composer's instructions were to perform the piece using the edge of the hand in a sideways chopping motion. "Chopsticks in Chinatown" should be played with a slight stop after each eighth note. In the melody (viola 2) part, the high A's should be played using the octave harmonic on the A string. Players who have not yet learned these harmonics could use open A instead of the harmonic.

Atacama Crossing

The Atacama desert is in Chile, stretching from the Pacific Ocean to the Andes Mountains, and receiving virtually no rainfall. Its desolate landscape has been described as "lunar". The Atacama Crossing is a 250-kilometer (150 mile) foot race across the Atacama desert, with competitors carrying all their own food, clothing, and gear. In "Atacama Crossing," leave the bow on the string during the rests, and prepare the new string level without making any sound.

Cross Lake Blues

Cross Lake is a town in the north of the Canadian province of Manitoba, situated on the lake called Cross Lake. In addition, there is a provincial park in Alberta, and a lake in the state of Maine in the U.S.A. with the same name. Use about half a bow, stopping the bow slightly after each note. In "Cross Lake Blues," prepare the string crossing while the bow rests silently on the string.

Darling River Monkey

The Darling River is the longest river in Australia, flowing across the south-eastern part of the country. It has a high salt content and a very irregular flow, some years drying up completely. Many teachers use "The Monkey Song" when teaching finger placement. "I'm a little monkey, climbing up a ladder, climbing to the top to pick a pink banana". This version of the monkey song has a two-beat rest for the student to prepare the left-hand fingers before playing the note. In "Darling River Monkey" the bow should remain silently on the string during the rest.

Athabasca Monkey

The Athabasca River begins in the Columbia Icefield of Jasper National Park, Alberta, Canada. It drains into Lake Athabasca and eventually into the Arctic Ocean. In the Cree language, the word "Athabasca" means "grass here and there". "Athabasca Monkey" is a transposition of "Darling River Monkey" to develop finger placement on the A string.

The cello versions of the monkey songs in *Magic Carpet* differ from the violin and viola versions, because most cello teachers begin finger placement by dropping all 4 fingers on the string and lifting them off one at a time, while most violin and viola teachers have their students do an ascending and descending pattern.

Machu Picchu Mountain

Machu Picchu is a ruined Inca city high on a mountain ridge in the Andes of Peru. Its name means "old peak" in the local Quechua language. Machu Picchu was likely built in the fifteenth century, and was re-discovered in 1911. It is sometimes called "the lost city of the Incas". "Machu Picchu Mountain" is a D major scale. As in the monkey songs, the bow should stay silently on the string during the rests while the left hand fingers are prepared.

Solos & Ensembles
by JOANNE MARTIN

Festive Strings

More Festive Strings

Folk Strings

More Folk Strings

FOR STRING QUARTET OR STRING ORCHESTRA:

(0906)	(0972)	**Violin 1**	(14680X)	(16030X)
(0911)	(0987)	**Violin 2**	(14760X)	(16110X)
(0912)	(0994)	**Violin 3**	(14840X)	(162X0)
(0927)	(0995)	**Viola**	(14920X)	(16380X)
(0985)	(0997)	**Cello**	(15060)	(16460X)
(0986)	(0998)	**Bass**	(15140X)	(16540X)
(0929)	(0971)	**Score**	(145X0)	(159X0)

FOR ENSEMBLES:

(0930)	(0973)	**Violin Ensemble**	(15220)	(16620X)
(0931)	(0974)	**Viola Ensemble**	(15300)	(16701X)
(0932)	(0975)	**Cello Ensemble**	(15490X)	(16890X)

FOR SOLO INSTRUMENTS:

(0933)	(0976)	**Solo Violin**	(15570X)	(16970X)
(0934)	(0977)	**Solo Viola**	(15650)	(17000X)
(0946)	(0978)	**Solo Cello**	(15730X)	(17190X)

PIANO ACCOMPANIMENT: (can be used in conjunction with all versions)

(0947)	(0979)	**Piano**	(15810)	(17270X)

PLUS

Trio Tapestry for Violin (17350X)
Trio Tapestry for Viola (17430X)
Trio Tapestry for Cello (17510X)
Trio Tapestry Piano Acc. (176X0)
ViolaFest, Volume 1 (0957)
Viola Fest, Volume 2 (0958)
Magic Carpet for Violin (27741)
Magic Carpet for Violin Piano Acc. (27012)
Magic Carpet for Viola (27744)
Magic Carpet for Viola Piano Acc. (27013)
Magic Carpet for Cello (27747)
Magic Carpet for Cello Piano Acc. (27014)

27013   US $6.95

0 38081 30297 3

SUMMY-BIRCHARD, INC.
Distributed by
Alfred Publishing Co., Inc.
alfred.com

SUMMY-BIRCHARD, INC.

ISBN 0-7390-4624-1

9 780739 046241

T2-BOE-060